THE VIBRATIONS OF LOVE

Trasha Nicole Hickman

Copyright © 2011 by Trasha Nicole Hickman

All rights reserved. Except as permitted under the U.S. Copyright Act of 1976, no part of this publication may be reproduced, distributed or transmitted in any form or by any means, or stored in a database or retrieval system without the prior permission of the author.

ISBN: 978-1-257-97907-3

Acknowledgments

To my Creator, for giving me the love of words and the gift of writing.

To my Mom, Doris J. Potter-Hickman, for encouraging me to read and recite poetry.

To my Dad, Rupert Hickman, for giving me the love of poetry.

To my Business Partner, Omar Seda, for for encouraging me to share my poems with the world.

To Esther and Jerry Hicks, for providing answers to questions that perplexed me.

To all my teachers, for the knowledge that they have imparted to me.

Contents

Introduction	1
Your Love	2
Seasons Of Love	4
You	5
Pleasure	6
Surrender	7
Emotions	8
Almost Doesn't Count	9
I May Not Understand	10
Wonder	12
Words I Can't Seem To Express	13
Within	14
The Day	15
Why	18

Longing	20
Tonight I Cried A Million Tears	21
Tonight I Cried	22
Because She Loves Him	23
Love	24
The Measure of Love	25
How Do You Love?	26
For The Love Of Grammar	27
I love	28
Unconditional Love	29
I love me	30
What Would You Do For Love?	31
For The Love Of	32
The Basis Of A Loving Relationship	33
Love Is	34
The Joy Of Love	35

How To Love Children?	36
The Journey Of Love	37
Waves Of Love	38
I Wish For You The Love Of	39
Love Is An Amazing Thing	40
Love Is The Highest Frequency	41
Conclusion	42

Introduction

Love is the highest frequency. Oh, the things we do for love. We often look for love in all the wrong places only to discover that what we were seeking could not be found in the places in which we were looking. Perhaps the love that we are seeking is the love from within. I was once told that when you find yourself you will find love! Love is steadfast, eternal and unchanging like the laws of the nature. I wish that I could capture all the multi-facets of love but to do so is to negate love. So without further ado, this book will take you on a journey through the frequency of love. It will take you to the highs of alignment and the lows of misalignment. Then it will reconnect you with the vibrations of love.

Your Love

Your love inspires me.
It inspires me to face my fears.

Your love challenges me.
It challenges me to confront all that I thought I knew.

Your love encourages me to be the best that I can.
Your love lifts me on days when I'm down.
It makes me believe that I can soar like a kite.

Your love makes me change for the better.
Your love is smooth like the jazz of Coltrane yet
hip like the songs of Sinatra.

Your love is beautiful as a ray of sun peering
through the clouds.
Your love is refreshing as the rain during the dog days of summer.

Your love is radiant.
It is as radiant as the smile of a child
on Christmas day.

Your love is joyous.
It is as joyous as the symphony filling my heart
with bliss.

Your love is timeless.
It is as timeless as eternity with
no beginning and no end.

Your love is playful.
It is as playful as little kittens frolicking
with a ball of yarn.

Your love is vast.
It is as vast as the universe.

Your love is liberating.
It is as liberating as a conviction
being overturned.

Your love is complicated.
It is as complicated as the most perplexing
mathematical equation.
Your love is all that I need and more.

Seasons Of Love

Shower me with your love in the spring.
Run with me in the summer.
Fall in love with me in the fall.
Take me in your loving arms in the winter.

You

You bring light into my life
You bring joy into my heart.
You bring music into my soul.
You bring a smile to my face.

Pleasure

Today I had the distinct pleasure of talking to a handsome fellow.
His mind was one I hope to make mine.
His love is one I hope to cherish and adore until the day I die.

Today I had the distinct pleasure of talking to an intellectual fellow.
A man that has a knack for solving other people's problems at the drop of a hat.

Today I had the distinct pleasure of conversing with a creative fellow.
His creativity parallels that of Einstein, Rockefeller, Yeats, Picasso and
all the other greats.

Today I had the distinct pleasure of talking to an honest fellow.
A man that is honest to a fault.

Today I had the distinct pleasure of talking to a loving fellow.
One who longed deeply for a requited love!

Today I had the distinct pleasure of talking to an enterprising fellow.
One who was on the verge of starting his second business.

Today I had the distinct pleasure of talking to the man I love beyond measure.

Surrender

I always thought that to surrender was a sign of weakness,
but today I surrendered to your love.

I always thought that to surrender was a sign of vulnerability,
but tonight I surrendered to your thoughts.

I spent my life vowing to never surrender to anyone
or anything but today I surrendered to your mind.

I always thought that to surrender meant that I was a weak person,
but tonight I surrendered to your love.

I promise you my love, my time, my devotion
and my faithfulness because I have decided to surrender to you.

I'm tired of fighting.
I'm tired of trying.
I'm tired of carrying the weight of the world on my shoulders.

Tonight, I decided to let you see the real me.
The person inside that I no longer want to hide.

Tonight I decided to surrender to your love and my life
will never be the same.

Emotions

Oh the joy that I feel is so inexplicable since I met you.
Oh the love that I feel is so immense that I'd give everything
I hold dear to be with you.
Oh the peace that I experience when I'm with you makes
me feel as though I'm in heaven.
Oh the faith that I exercise with you daily
let's me know that I'm growing by leaps and bounds.
Oh the courage that I have to muster when we are apart
is a harrowing feat.
Oh the emptiness that I feel when you are away leaves
me feeling incomplete.

Almost Doesn't Count

I almost had a wonderful fulfilling relationship.

I almost shared my personal thoughts, feelings and emotions.

I almost committed to loving you and you only.

I almost became everything that you wanted me to be.

I almost became the person I dreamed of becoming with the man of my dreams.

But almost doesn't count.

I almost loved you with all my heart, with all my soul, with all my strength, but almost doesn't count.

I almost lived the life I had imaged, but almost doesn't count.

I almost obtain everything that I wanted in this life, but almost doesn't count.

I almost most ended up with you, but almost doesn't count.

I almost gave you my life, but almost doesn't count.

I May Not Understand

I may not understand
why you do the
things that you do.

Why you stay
when I want you to leave.

I may not understand
why you care for me so
much.

I've caused you such
heartache and pain.

I may not understand
why you are so forgiving
when I've done
hurtful things
over and over.

I may not understand
why you love me the
way you do.

When I have done
so many things
wrong.

I may not understand
why you wanted
me to be your wife.

When in the end,
all I wanted was
a friend.

I may not understand
but I'm thankful
that you
cared,
thankful
that you were
forgiving,
thankful
that you love
me for me.

I may not understand
thee,
but I am thankful.

Wonder

I wonder do you ever think of me.
I wonder do you ever dream of walking hand and hand barefoot on the sand.

I wonder do you ever think of me the way I think of you.
I wonder do you dream of holding me close.

I wonder do you feel the same way that I feel about you.
I wonder if you ever dream of staring deep into my eyes.
I wonder do you realize that half the time I have things I want to say to you, but I don't know how to express them.
I wonder do you realize that I care very much for you, but
I'm not sure how to show you that I care.

Words I Can't Seem To Express

I try to find the words to explain how I feel but they always seem to elude me.
I try to express my feelings, yet I always feel as though I fumble with what I have to say.
I try to communicate the thoughts that race through my mind but somehow they seem to dissipate when I talk to you.

Feelings of fear, confusion, and anxiety bombard my mind.
Feelings of vulnerability and loneliness overwhelm my heart.
Feelings of innocence and naivety torment my soul.

As I watch the days of my life slip by like the sand in an hour glass,
I wonder will I ever express my feelings to you,
or will I have to live with regrets wondering what may have been or could have been all because I can't express my feelings to you.

Within

Somewhere deep within the recesses of my mind
I dream of a distant place and time.

I dream of a love that was forbidden.

I dream of a love that I had to keep hidden.

Somewhere deep within the recesses of my mind
I dream of a love that I could only dream was mine.

A love that was timid, shy and brand new.

One in which I didn't know what to do.

Somewhere deep within the recesses of my mind
I dream of a distant place and time where we could
go far away some place where no one would know.

Somewhere deep with the recesses of my mind
I dream of a distance place and time a time where
I could share my feelings with you.

A place where there was no one but me and you.

Somewhere deep within the recesses of my mind
lives a love that water cannot extinguish and
commandments cannot separate.

Somewhere deep within the recesses of my mind.

The Day

One day our paths intersected
and my life was changed forever.
You were amazed by the qualities
and characteristics that I could not see.

You were astound by my patience,
compassion, honesty, and virtues.
You said that what you saw in me
was what you asked God for in a
wife.

One day our paths intersected
and my life was changed forever.
I told you that I felt different,
peculiar and misunderstood.
You told me that I was special.

One day our paths intersected
and my life was changed
forever.
I used to hold my head down
when I walked.

You told me that one day
I would not hold my head
down anymore.

One day our paths intersected
and my life was changed
forever.

You gave me love that I
did not know how to receive.
You gave me gifts and I was
suspect of your motives.

One day our paths intersected
and my life was changed forever.
You expressed your feelings to
me and at that time I felt my heart
was made of stone.

You told me you loved me
and I did not respond.
So afraid of getting hurt and
so afraid of letting anyone
get too close to me.

One day our paths intersected
and my life was changed forever.
You tried to surprise me and I
was not able to receive your love.
I told you I thought we should
be friends. I broke your heart.

Now that our relationship is
not what it use to be, I'm beginning
to realize what an indelible print
you have left on my heart.

The heart that was once so cold
is soft and fragile as a snow flake.
I now hold my head high when I
walk.

I no longer think something
is wrong with me because
I'm different and because people
misunderstand me.

I count it as a blessing.
Now I express my feelings
in ways that I never knew
that I could.

You once asked me if I loved you.
I told you yes I loved you, yet
I don't think I truly knew
what it meant to love someone.

You have taught we what it
truly means to love someone.
I truly understand that love involves
longsuffering and sacrifice.
You bear the scars on your heart for
all the things you had to endure in
dealing with me.

Thank you for your love.
Thank you for loving me for me.
Thank you for accepting me for
who I am and not trying to change
me.

One day our paths intersected and
my life was changed forever.

Why

Why do I long to be with you after two years of hell?
Why do I wish I could hear your voice again?
Why do I wish I could see your smile when I know that everything wasn't peaches and cream?

Why do I long to be held by you when I feared you so much?
Why did I have to fall deeply in love with you?
Why did I have to allow you into my world?

Because even though you are gone I can't seem to get you out of my head and my heart.

Why do I miss you so?
Why is there a man in my life who loves me
and I still wish that you were him?

Why did I have to fall deeply in love with you?
They say that time heals all wounds but I'm
not sure that that is true.
It's been two years since I left you and I miss you so much.

Why do I miss you?
I was afraid to be around you when we were a couple.
Why are you a part of my soul?
I fear that I may never get over you.

Why did I have to fall deeply for you?
Because now it wouldn't be so challenging
getting over you.

Why did I not say the things that I was afraid to say when
I had the chance?
Why did I allow fear to control my destiny?

Why did I allow other people's opinion of your
actions change my perception of you?

Why didn't I love you for you and not
try to create you in my own image?

Why did I turn another year old and wonder
did you remember that it was my birthday?

Why do I have so many questions left unanswered and
a void in my soul?

Why did I have to go and fall for you because I
have never fallen for anyone before?

Why did I abuse you and fail to appreciate you for you?
Why have I been trying to suppress, repress and deny
that I don't care for you still?
Why do I feel all these things when our relationship
had more turbulence than an airplane flying in the sky?

Why did I give my heart and soul and still feel as though I'm a failure?
Why did I have to fall in love with you?

Why?

Longing

I long to be in your presence again.
I long to talk to you again.
I long to listen to the events that have
transpired in your day.

Ironic I regret the day that I left you.
I regret that I feared telling you
what was in my heart.

I am sadden often by the fact that
I allowed fear to control my actions
and caused me to act obnoxious.

I long to accompany you to your recitals
although I'm not versed in music.

Some days I long to hear your voice.
Some days I long to touch your hand
and spend quality time with you.

You may never feel the way I feel
but it's ironic that I long for you still.

I wish I took the time to be present for the
things that meant so much to you.
I regret that I was absence because I
was afraid.
It's ironic that after three years of
departing from your life
I long for you still.

Tonight I Cried A Million Tears

Tonight I cried a million tears because once again I felt abandoned.

I cried a million tears because years were wasted.

I cried a million tears because I tried to leave earlier, but you insisted that I stay.

I cried a million tears that somehow don't fade away.

Tonight I cried a million tears because I was left to pick up the pieces again.

Tonight I cried a million tears because I wondered will it ever end.

Tonight I cried a million tears and no one will know but me.

I guess I cried a million tears to get over thee.

Tonight I Cried

Tonight I cried immensely because I realized I've never loved anyone.
Tonight I cried deeply because what I thought was love was fear, control and manipulation.
Tonight I cried because I've left a path of destruction, broken hearts and empty promises.
Tonight I cried because I realized I'm not able to discern love from control and possessiveness.
Tonight I cried because somehow everything I thought was true was an illusion.
Tonight I cried because I realized the only person who rejected me was me.
Tonight I cried immensely for all those I've hurt.
Tonight I cried for me because somehow I lost me.

Because She Loves Him

Because she loves him she feels joy.
Because she loves him she looks forward to
each new day.
Because she loves him she can overcome any
obstacle.
Because she loves him she can face her fears.
Because she loves him she can express herself.
Because she loves him she can be faithful to him.
Because she loves him she loves him more than he will
ever know.

Love

Love.............my joy
Love.........my hope
Love.......my refuge
Love.........my friend
Love....my redemption
Love....my solace
Love........my partner
Love.......my dream
Love.........my artist
Love........my mentor
Love......my biggest fan
Love the best of me
Love the worst of me
Love is all that I am
and all that I am not.

The Measure Of Love

It is often said that we should love each other unconditionally.
Yet often time we put so many restrictions and conditions on love.

The true measure of love is not how we love others or how others
love us when we live up to their expectations, ideas, beliefs or images of
us.

The true measure of love is how they love us when we fail to live up to
their beliefs.

The true measure of love is how they love us when we seek to find our own
voice or claim our own space even if it means breaking with ideas,
concepts, paradigms and attitudes that we were inculcated to believe.

To live one's life on one's own terms and to define one's own life
that's the true measure of love.

How do you love me when I am not what you want me to be?
How do you love me when I choose to see the world from a
different point of view than you?

How do you love me when I no longer hold sacrosanct all the things
everyone told me were true?

How Do You Love?

How do you love?

I have pondered this question many times.
To love without being devastated.
To risk without losing it all.

How do you love deeply and remain sane?
How do you show that you care without caring too much?
How do you love without losing touch?

Touch with yourself, your dreams, desires, hopes and aspiration.

How do you love?
How do you give without giving too much?

How do you love?
Love yourself?

How do you love?

For The Love of Grammar

Part I

I love nouns.
I love verbs.
I love most things with words.
I love that I comes before E except after C.

Part II

I love subjects.
I love verbs.
I love the power of words.
I love sentences that don't end in prepositions.

Part III

I love conjunctions and the functions they serve.
I love adverbs and the way they modify words.
I love words!

I love

I love the sound of rustling leaves blowing in the breeze.
I love the sight of stars twinkling at night.
I love the smell of flowers in bloom half past noon.
I love the taste of fruit in an unaltered state.
I love the feel of snowflakes landing in my hand.

Unconditional Love

I love you when you make mistakes.
I love you when you are self-destructive.
I love you though you have no idea what normal means.
I love you when things seem to go wrong.
I love you when the days are dark and dreary.
I love you when the nights are long.
I love you when you are right, and I love you when you are wrong.
I love you when it is raining, and I love you when the sun is shining.
I love you when it sleets, and I love you when it snows.
I love you today, and I will love you tomorrow.
I love you when you are sad, and I will love you through your sorrows.
I love you when you laugh, and I love you when you play.
I will always love you no matter what.

I love me

I love me with the ease of birds gliding through the sky.
I love me with the grace of the earth rotating on its axis.
I love me perpetually like life itself.
I love me majestically like the sun setting in the evening.
I love me effortlessly like the ebb and flow of the tide.
I love me endlessly like eternity.
I love me unconditionally like love itself.
I love me joyfully like squirrels jumping from tree to tree.
I love me with the awe of snow dangling in the trees.
I love me like consciousness flowing through my mind with ease.
I love me like a kind word spoken at the appropriate time.
I love me…

What Would You Do For Love?

What would you do for love?
Would you leave a job that you have outgrown to follow your heart?
Would you end a relationship that was no longer working for you to create one that is a perfect match?

What would you do for love?
What would you say?
What would you do?
What would you refrain from doing for love?

Would you learn something new?
Would you change?
Would you remain the same?

What would you do for love?

For The Love Of....

For the love of creating, believe that all things are possible.
For the love of words, speak only what you want to experience.
For the love of peace of mind, direct your thoughts.
For the love of self, follow your passion.
For the love of success, learn the natural laws.
For the love of thoughts, expect the best.
For the love of consciousness, raise your vibrations.

The Basis Of A Loving Relationship

The basis of any relationship is trust and communication.

Where there is no trust and communication there can be no relationship.

Forgiveness must be at the heart of any relationship
in order for it to thrive and grow.

We don't pay for our sins.

We make mistakes, we ask for forgiveness, we receive grace
and mercy we move on and we have fun.

Focus on your partner's strengths not weakness.
Love your partner of who he or she is.
Don't try to change him or her.

Love Is

Love is eternal.
Love is sublime.
Love is manifesting its universal mind.
Love is free.
Love is forgiving.
Love is constant.
Love is stable.
Love is willing.
Love is able.
Love is here.
Love is there.
Love is everywhere.
Love is energy in motion.
Love is vibrations in motion.
Love is creative.
Love is the beginning.
Love is the end.
Love is expressing itself in different forms my friend.
Love is uplifting.
Love is inspiring.
Love is desiring.
Love is sustaining.
Love is forever reigning supreme.
Love is the zest of life.
Love is consciousness.
Love is seeing the best and expecting the best in any and everything.
Love Is…

The Joy Of Love

The joy of love is changing and evolving.
The joy of love makes your heart sing.
The joy of love is life giving.
The joy of love is knowing that freedom reigns supreme.
The joy of love is creating and innovating.
The joy of love is unlimited and abundant.
The joy of love is knowing all is well.
The joy of love is uplifting.
The joy of love elevates consciousness.
The joy of love raises your vibrations.

How To Love Children?

Let children live their lives.

Don't compare them at all.

Honor their feelings even if they seem small.

Be present for them.

Teach them to be independent and think independently.

Affirm children's hopes, dreams and goals so that their lives may unfold

in the way that they imagine.

Encourage their imagination.

Allow them the freedom to dream.

Teach them how to direct their words and thoughts.

Encourage them to always see the sunny side of life
and teach them the power of positive thinking.

The Journey Of Love

Somewhere in a distance place and time love decided to take shape and form.
To experience life anew, from a different point of view.
As love traveled on its journey through this plane, one thing remained the same love came for the joy of expressing itself.
And while on its journey through this plane, love came to answer questions that were posed and to provide solutions to problems that arose to make life better.
And when love decides that it no longer wants to reside in this plane and experience life from a certain point of view it reemerges to begin anew.

Waves Of Love

Waves of love come and go.
Some stay for a lifetime.
Some stay for a while.
Some come to make us smile.

Waves of love are present always
to remind us that there are always better days.

And if you think you missed a wave of love
don't worry another one will be sent from up above.

Waves of love are the epitome of light shining
through to illuminate sight.

Waves of love are the highest frequency
and the ones we have been seeking
and the ones we all hope to be.

I Wish For You The Love Of....

I wish for you the love of a poet who expresses herself eloquently.
I wish for you the love of the sun that shines abundantly.
I wish for you the love of the wind that moves freely.
I wish for you the love of a snowflake that is pure.
I wish for you the love of a child that is honest and forgiving.
I wish for you the love of the rain that is refreshing after a scorching day.
I wish for you the love of chasing the sun and realizing how fun chasing dreams can be.

I wish for you the love of alignment where everything falls into place at the precise time.
I wish for you the love of presence of being present in the moment.
I wish for you the love of ease that come with following your heart.

I wish for you the love of faith that nothing is impossible.
I wish for you the love of peace of mind that comes when you are aligned.
I wish for you the love of inspiration that nourishes your soul.
I wish for you the love of creativity in whatever forms it manifest.

I wish for you love that is unconditional that emanates from the creator.

Love Is An Amazing Thing

Love is an amazing thing it powers all our hopes and dreams.
It lights our paths and serves as a guide.

Love is everlasting and a constant throughout the ages.
It is forever summoning us to reach for higher frequencies.
It refuses to see anything less than the best of you and me.

It is amazing all the manifestations of love too numerous to count
like stars up above.

Love invites us to open our heart for with each passing moment
we are afforded a new start.

Love requires nothing in exchange for all the things it gives us
and love is willing at any moment to forever forgive us.

Love Is The Highest Frequency

Love is the highest frequency.
It resonates throughout time and space.

Love is the highest frequency.
It never dips.
It never changes.
It remains the same throughout the ages.

Love is the highest frequency.
It beckons us to match its wavelength.

Love is the highest frequency.
It is energy in motion.
It is consciousness.
It is awareness.
It is God.
It has always been and forever will be.

Love is the highest frequency.
It is multidimensional.
It encourages us to align to all that is divine.

Love is the highest frequency.
It is the purest vibrations that can be calibrated.

The vibrations of love are the highest frequency.

May the love of energy illuminate your path, may the love of your passion take you to your dreams and may the vibrations of love forever reign supreme.

Love,

Trasha Nicole Hickman

www.ingramcontent.com/pod-product-compliance
Lightning Source LLC
Chambersburg PA
CBHW022345040426
42449CB00006B/725